D0996390

CHANDLER'S FORD
A Pictorial History

The site of the ford in Leigh Road, as it appeared in the early years of this century. The photograph is taken looking towards Eastleigh.

CHANDLER'S FORD
A Pictorial History

Barbara Hillier

Phillimore

1994

Published by
PHILLIMORE & CO. LTD.,
Shopwyke Manor Barn, Chichester, West Sussex

ISBN 0 85033 896 4

Printed and bound in Great Britain by
BIDDLES LTD.
Guildford, Surrey

List of Illustrations

Acknowledgements

Thanks are due to the following people who have assisted in the production of this book: Ann Currall (Librarian at Chandler's Ford Library) for locating a number of photographs and organising the copying of them. Frank Dovey for producing copies of a number of the photographs which have been added to my collection and appear in this book. Jo Ann Hillier for typing the original manuscript. Elaine Howells for preparing the final manuscript for publication.

To the following people who were the original donors of the photographs which appear in this book: Mrs. V. Baker, 109; Mrs. A. Barrett, 11, 24, 33, 83; Mr. W. Biddlecombe, 44, 55, 65, 66, 123, 135, 136, 159; Mr. Brown, 94, 95; Mrs. I. Cant, 115; Chandler's Ford Library, 1-4, 6, 9, 10, 12, 13, 15, 25, 37, 42, 48, 68, 87, 112, 141, 152, 153, 158 (Mr. G. Cox), 39, 53, 76 (Mr. Ely), 70, 71 (Mrs. Higgins), 58 (Mrs. Kruse), 90, 142 (Miss Wise), 120-22; Mrs. Crumplin, 72, 73, 139; Mr. R. Dean, 35, 46, 78, 79, 80-82, 88; Mrs. R. Dore, 101; Mr. N. Dowell, 69; *Eastleigh Weekly News*, 14, 22, 28, 29, 34, 62, 102; Mr. R. Gilham, 30; Mrs. Goater, 16; Mrs. Goddard, 54; Hampshire County Record Office, 5, 7, 8, 40, 41, 47; Mrs. K. Hilary, 36, 103-6, 108, 124, 125, 128, 130, 154-56; Mrs. E. Hillier, frontispiece, 18-21, 23, 27, 43, 51, 57, 59, 60, 61, 74, 91-93, 96-100, 110, 114, 116-18, 126, 129, 132, 140, 143, 144, 149, 150, 157; Mrs. Holt, 67, 77; Miss J. Horn, 75, 119, 138, 147; Mr. M. Jackson, 32; Mr. Mitchell, 38; Mr. W. Munckton, 85, 86; Mrs. M. Newton, 17, 49, 50, 131, 133, 134, 137; Mrs. P. O'Brien, 113, 160; Mr. L. Peach, 31, 45, 56, 89, 107; Mr. G. Piper 26, 63, 64, 84, 111, 145, 148, 151; Mrs. D. Pryce, 52; Mr. and Mrs. A. Webb, 127, 146.

Introduction

For hundreds of years, the area now known as Chandler's Ford was a stretch of countryside much akin to that of the New Forest. It contained the same variety of habitats: mixed woodland, heathland and wet meadow. A number of brooks and streams flowed through the area, to merge together and finally join with the River Itchen. Bronze Age man lived in the northern part, and no fewer than eleven tumuli were excavated by the Hampshire Field Club at the end of the last century, when urns containing the ashes of the cremated dead were taken for display at the Hartley Institute Museum in Southampton.

Three fords existed on tracks which later became the major roads of the village; one on the main Winchester-Southampton road, one on Hursley Road, and one on Leigh Road. The village acquired part of its name from either the ford on the Winchester-Southampton road or that on the Hursley Road, but the origin of the 'Chandler's' part remains a mystery, the spelling having changed several times over the centuries, and no positive documentation has been found.

During the latter part of the 16th and the first few years of the 17th centuries, farms and farm workers' cottages were built, belonging to Hursley Park Estates and the Manor of North Stoneham. Hiltonbury Farm was probably the earliest of these, the original building appearing on a map of 1588. The building has an interesting history, being developed and added to over the years. The distinctive chimneys are a Victorian addition, and these and other features are repeated on a number of buildings which were owned by Hursley Park Estates at this time. In the 1890s, Hiltonbury Farm was sold to Cranbury Park Estates, and remained in their ownership until it ceased to be a working farm in the late 1970s. The farmhouse remains as a public house, in the centre of the North Miller's Dale housing development, built on what had previously been the farmland.

The workers at Hiltonbury Farm were housed in thatched cottages at Ramalley and in Cuckoo Bushes Lane. Only one of these cottages now remains. At the top of Ramalley Lane, there was originally a group of seven or eight of these cottages, for which the tenants in 1740 paid five shillings per annum in rent. In 1638, Richard Major, a son of the Mayor of Southampton, acquired the Great Lodge of Hursley Park, and the accompanying Hursley Estates. In 1649, his daughter, Dorothy, married Richard Cromwell, third but eldest surviving son of Oliver Cromwell, and the young couple lived with Dorothy's father at Hursley. It is recorded that they attended the 'Merrie Feast', which was held annually at Ramalley, 'merries' being the small, sweet cherries which grew plentifully in the area, were harvested, and sold at this annual social event. The 'Merrie Feasts' were a feature of local country life for almost two hundred years.

Ford Farm in Hursley Road was another early farm established in the Chandler's Ford area, as were Titlark, Velmore and Hut Farms on the main Southampton Road, and North End Farm in what is now Oakmount Road. These farms, with their accompanying cottages, belonged to the Manor of North Stoneham. By 1850, this small community, scattered across the whole area known as Chandler's Ford, amounted to a total population of something just under two hundred.

As the main Winchester-Southampton road passes through Chandler's Ford it follows a route which is very close to, and almost parallel with, the Roman road from Nursling to Winchester. Evidence of the Roman road has been found in recent times when excavations were taking place for new housing, for the Wessex Nuffield Hospital, and for the Pitmore and Thornden schools. The main road between the two major cities of Winchester and Southampton has always been a busy thoroughfare, from the time of foot travellers and stage-coaches to the present day. Stage-coaches from Southampton to London passed through regularly, and this led to the building of the first bridge over the ford in the late 18th century. In the early 19th century, two toll-gates were built, one marked by a house on the corner of what is now Leigh Road, and the other at Fryern Hill, opposite to the present site of the *Halfway Inn*. In 1829, the tolls collected at these two gates amounted to £495. Behind the Fryern Hill toll-house were stables at which the horses were changed, and a smithy.

In 1847, the Salisbury branch of the London and South Western Railway was opened, and the station at Chandler's Ford became operative on 22 November in that year. At this time, it was simply a 'halt', used mainly by the family at Hursley Park House. In 1866, the body of John Keble, Hursley's famous 19th-century vicar, was brought back from Bournemouth by train to Chandler's Ford station and taken to Hursley for burial. During his lifetime, he had been a regular traveller from the station, but the story that he wrote his famous hymn, *Sun of my Soul*, whilst waiting there for a train is sadly only a local legend.

The first really significant development in Chandler's Ford's growth as a village in the 19th century was the establishment of a flourishing brick-making industry. This began around 1870, and continued to thrive until the outbreak of the First World War. There were small brickyards at Scantabout and on the northern side of Common Road, but the centre of the industry was the brickyard, reputed to be one of the largest in the country, which stretched from the railway along the main Southampton Road, almost as far as Castle Lane. It is interesting that today's Industrial Estate, the main focus of Chandler's Ford's 20th-century light industry, occupies the same site.

The bricks produced were used for local building in Chandler's Ford and the rapidly expanding railway town of Eastleigh, and also for Eastleigh's Railway Carriage Works. The most famous consignment of bricks was that of three million which was transported to London for the building of the Courts of Justice in The Strand. Terraced and semi-detached cottages were built to house the brickworkers and their families, some of which remain today including a terrace on Bournemouth Road, the end building of which was the first post office.

In 1892, Mrs. Mary Wallis bought the Brownhill Estate in Chandler's Ford from the trustees of the late Sir William Heathcote of Hursley Park and laid it out for building purposes. This purchase took place as a result of her sale of a package of land in Eastleigh, to be developed for the Railway Works. In 1894, Mr. and Mrs. Wallis built and moved into King's Court at Fryern Hill, a house that survives today as the Masonic headquarters, and the lodge of which has been extended and made into the King's Court Restaurant.

The mixture of late Victorian housing evident today in parts of Brownhill Road, Park Road, Valley Road and Hursley Road, came about as a result of the development of the Brownhill Estate. Mr. Wallis also extolled the charms of Chandler's Ford to a number of his friends and acquaintances, referring to it as an 'inland Bournemouth', and a 'charming neighbourhood with a salubrious climate', and this led to a number of more substantial houses being built around the area, including Terriote, Merdon and Merrieleas.

Throughout the 19th century, the village had been quite clearly divided between the three parishes of Otterbourne, Hursley and North Stoneham, but on 1 October 1897, Chandler's Ford's first Parish Council was formed. It became a separate parish in its own right, comprised of parts of North and South Stoneham, Ampfield, North Baddesley and Otterbourne, and this new parish was taken over by the Hursley Rural District Council. By 1900, the population of the village had grown to around a thousand.

The last two decades of the 19th century saw the people of Chandler's Ford developing all the amenities necessary for life in a growing village.

In 1881, the Anglican worshippers built their first small church, having held services up to this point in the home of Mr. Wren, and led by Mr. Wynyard of Hursley. The first church was built of corrugated iron, and stood behind the site of the present post office in Bournemouth Road. It was opened on Good Friday 1881, and the following year was moved to a site in Hursley Road, close to that of the present St Boniface church. By 1888, a larger building was needed and the first mission church of St Boniface was erected, again on the Bournemouth Road site. It was also built of corrugated iron and was known affectionately as the 'Iron Church'. The original church was moved back to stand beside it. The present St Boniface church was built on land in Hursley Road given by Mr. Tankerville Chamberlayne of Cranbury Park. It was dedicated by the bishop of Winchester on 4 October 1904, but remained under the jurisdiction of the Parish of North Stoneham until 1910, when its first vicar, the Rev. R Pierssene, was inducted.

The first non-conformist church to appear in Chandler's Ford was the Primitive Methodist chapel in Brownhill Road, now the Age Concern Hall. A group of enthusiastic non-conformists had met for a number of years in a cottage at Fryern Hill, and held open air services; but it was not until 1900, under the leadership of Rev. Stewart Hooson of Eastleigh, that the Methodist chapel was built. The building was of bricks produced in Chandler's Ford, it cost £400 to build, including the price of the land, and it could seat 120 people. For the first years of its life, the chapel's small congregation had to hold many fund-raising events in their struggle to pay off their debt, a feat which was not accomplished until 1924.

The first school in Chandler's Ford was held in the original corrugated iron room, which was also the church. Miss Isabel Laidlaw was the first schoolmistress and was paid a salary of £50 per annum. By 1892, larger premises were needed, and the school managers appealed to all the residents of the village to raise the required sum of £800. The new school was opened in 1893, on the main Southampton road, near to its junction with what is still appropriately named School Lane. Mr. Bocking was the first headteacher but he remained for only two years, being succeeded by Mrs. Cleall, who was appointed in 1895 on a salary of £90 per annum. She gained the reputation of being an over-strict disciplinarian and was forced into resignation in 1905 due to the harshness of her treatment of one of the pupils from the Hursley Union Workhouse.

Her successor was Mr. Howse, who remained in his post for 20 years. He was an enlightened village schoolmaster for his time, and had a reputation for leading his pupils in field studies for both local and natural history. His school was visited by student teachers in training in order that they might see the apparatus made by Mr. Howse and his pupils to assist them in their scientific experiments. He also played a leading rôle in village life, organising fêtes and fairs, and master-minding, in 1919, the first of many village carnivals.

Before the turn of the century, the new school was too small for its expanding population and an infant class of 50 pupils had to return to the old 'iron room'. Hampshire County Council applied increasing pressure on the school managers to provide an adequate building for the education of the infants, but despite several appeals the church was unable to meet the financial demands, and when the new infant school was opened in King's Road in 1908, it was a school funded and run by the Hampshire County Council. The previous school then became the 'Senior' school, to which pupils transferred at the age of eight or nine.

School records reflect much of the life of the ordinary villagers of this pre-First World War period, describing childhood epidemics, poverty, and rural pursuits. Many children were unable to attend school in bad weather through lack of shoes and outer clothing. Still more took time off to help with the brickmaking, haymaking, hop-picking and acorn-gathering, and to act as beaters for the shooting parties from Cranbury Park.

Horse-racing is the first sport recorded in the records of Chandler's Ford. The Chandler's Ford and South Hants. Steeplechases were held at Titlark Farm from 1883 to 1885, and attracted crowds from many surrounding villages. By 1914, cricket and football teams were well established, as were a rifle club and a Brass and Reed Band, adding to the recreational activities of the villagers. An early Scout Group was run by Mr. Tuersley, the postmaster, who had taken over the new post office built at the end of Hursley Road in 1900.

The establishment of public houses and shopping facilities were further signs of the developing village. In 1870, the *Halfway Inn* was built at Fryern Hill, the first landlord being Mr. Ham Rodaway, who had previously kept a small general shop in what is now Oakmount Road. Appearing in the 1841 census, this shop was the first to be recorded in the village. Hut Farm, built in 1730 behind the present site of the Hendy Ford showrooms on Bournemouth Road, had always brewed and sold beer in a small side building known as the New Hut. The *Hut Hotel* was built nearby in 1894, and was quite a grand hostelry for its day, with stabling for horses and accommodation for travellers. The *Railway Hotel* was built near the station in 1898 to provide refreshment for those arriving by train, but with the closing of the station in 1969, the name became obsolete and it is now called the *Monk's Brook*. One of Chandler's Ford's best known shops today is that of F. H. Dean and Son, selling a range of hardware and gardening equipment. Mr. Albert Dean began the business in 1906 in one of a pair of shops in Hursley Road on the corner of Ramalley Lane. His contemporaries in the shop-keeping business ran the first newsagents, butchers, bakers and a small co-operative store. The latter, together with Lloyds Bank, were housed in a row of shops, never to be completed, at the end of Hursley Road. The First World War brought the building of these shops to an abrupt halt.

The village did not escape evidence of the hostilities of 1914-18. Soldiers marching from Winchester to board the troopships at Southampton rested on the Green at Fryern Hill, the present site of Safeways. School children had unexpected holidays when the noise of thirty to forty thousand troops marching close to the school made lessons impossible. The re-mount horses based at Cranbury Park frequently exercised through the village. Women were seen doing unfamiliar jobs such as working on the roads and delivering mail.

Celebrations were held on Saturday 26 July 1919, when peace finally returned. An open-air service was followed by a dinner for all demobilised men and their families, and then a grand procession, led by the Brass and Reed Band, took the villagers to Hut Farm. Here, the children were presented with Peace Medals and given tea in the barn. By this time, it was raining heavily and the celebrations concluded a week later with a bonfire and fireworks display.

The real toll of the war for the people of the village is recorded by the names on the War Memorial: 47 men and one woman, Margaret Caswall, lost their lives. The Memorial was unveiled on 6 March 1920 by Major Hennessey, M.P. The Archdeacon of Winchester led prayers and Mr. Carpenter read the Roll of Honour. At first, the War Memorial stood at the end of Hursley Road, but has now been moved to stand outside St Boniface church.

The twenty years between the two World Wars saw the population of Chandler's Ford increase to over 3,000. In the 1920s, the land belonging to King's Court, Merdon House and Hut Farm were all sold for building development, as was some of the land in the Hiltingbury area.

Changes and developments took place to meet the requirements of the ever-increasing population. St Boniface church added the chancel to the original building, moved the belfry to the west end of the building and installed an organ. These additions were dedicated on 15 December 1929. The Methodist congregation added a side room extension to their chapel, a porch over the main door and a small kitchen. These extensions were opened in 1937.

A retired Congregational minister, the Rev. Lloyd Jones, had been holding services in his home and he led the group of people who founded the Congregational church in Chandler's Ford. It was built in King's Road and was opened on 17 October 1929. In 1937, St Edward's Roman Catholic church was built on Winchester Road, as an offering of thanks by Edward and Helen Christian of Otterbourne Manor, thus completing the range of Christian denominations represented in the village.

The Infant School in King's Road increased its accommodation by the addition of 'huts' as classrooms, but the church found the expense of running the Senior School an increasing burden, and it finally closed in 1939, when the new North End Secondary Modern School opened in Leigh Road. Pupils who passed the Scholarship Examination in the 1920s and '30s continued their education at Barton Peveril Grammar School.

Sherborne House School, a private school founded by Mrs. Wise, opened in 1933 in a house in Park Road and then moved to its current location in Lakewood Road.

The general atmosphere of the village was still very rural in these pre-war days, but new shopping areas were built at Fryern Hill and Bournemouth Road, and recreational facilities continued to develop. In 1914, the Ritchie Hall had been opened, next to St Boniface church. It had been given by Mrs. Ritchie as a memorial to her husband who had been the local doctor for 15 years. He had also been choirmaster, lay reader and Secretary of the Winchester Diocesan Choral Union. The modern Community Association buildings have now been added at the Ritchie Hall, forming a complex of rooms for local events.

In pre-war times, whist-drives and dances were held, and the first Women's Institute and Girls' Friendly Society were formed by Miss Kennedy. The cricket and football teams continued to flourish; there was a tennis club; the first Brownies and Girl Guides were started by Mrs. Hignett; a carnival was held annually; the Bands continued and a Choral Society was formed. The Central Club and Institute was built in the 1920s.

Infectious diseases, and in particular the scourge of tuberculosis, affected many families. An Isolation Hospital, now demolished, was built in 1912 on open land off Oakmount Road, and in 1921 the Hursley Union Workhouse became a sanatorium for tuberculosis sufferers. The Workhouse had been built in 1900, in Cuckoo Bushes Lane, and the building survives today as Leigh House, a psychiatric unit for adolescents.

A major administrative change came about in 1932 when Chandler's Ford, and parts of Otterbourne, North Stoneham, Fair Oak and Stoke Park, were removed from the surrounding Rural Districts and joined to the Eastleigh and Bishopstoke Urban District. The last meeting of Chandler's Ford Parish Council was held on 29 March 1932. The new Urban District Council was created a Municipal Borough by His Majesty King Edward VIII on 4 August 1936, and Chandler's Ford became a ward of Eastleigh Borough Council.

It seems incredible today that a village so close to the devastated city of Southampton should have suffered little direct effect of enemy action in the Second World War. The reflection of the fires in the stricken city could be clearly seen in the night sky, but only two of the stray bombs to fall in the area immediately surrounding Chandler's Ford caused any loss of life.

Early in the war, evacuees from Portsmouth increased the number of pupils in the school, as did the arrival of families who were later bombed out of their Southampton homes. In 1941, the number on roll rose by over 100, and the numbers in individual classes ranged from 38 to 47. Schooling was also disrupted by over 250 daytime air raid warnings during the first years of the war.

During the first daylight air attack on Southampton, when German bomber escorts were trying to fight off Spitfires and Hurricanes, a Messerschmitt Me-110 crashed in a field in Baddesley Road. The pilot parachuted into the grounds of Cranbury Park and was taken prisoner by the Otterbourne Home Guard, but his rear gunner died in the crash. He was buried in the Hursley churchyard but his remains were exhumed in 1969 and re-interred in Germany.

Prior to the D-Day landings, an estimated 10,000 troops were encamped in the village, mainly in the area between Hiltingbury Road and Hocombe Road. Army transport vehicles blocked every road and track except the main Winchester-Southampton road and Hursley Road. Official passes were issued to the few families who lived in this part of the village, and in the final days some were confined to their homes in order to ensure complete secrecy regarding troop movements.

There are still a number of families in the Eastleigh and Chandler's Ford area who are of Polish descent. Many of them came first to live at the Polish refugee camp in Pine Road, which was established towards the end of the war and remained until the 1950s.

Since the Second World War, the whole character and environment of Chandler's Ford has changed, due to housing developments, so that by the late 1980s the population figure was approaching 25,000.

The western side of Hursley Road was the first sign of post-war development in the mid-1950s, and this was followed rapidly by housing across the whole of Hiltingbury, Scantabout, Peverells Wood and the Springhill and Oakmount areas. Individual meadows disappeared under houses, large houses were demolished and small 'closes' built, the Velmore area was developed and the land surrounding Hiltonbury Farm became the North and South Miller's Dale housing estates. More recently, the whole new 'village' of Valley Park has appeared on the western side of Monk's Brook.

Each new housing complex has led to the building of accompanying shops, public houses and schools. Eight schools now cater for the primary phase of education, and they, in turn, feed into two comprehensive schools. As well as local shops for each phase of housing, the Central Precinct was built at the end of Hursley Road, followed in the mid-1960s by the Fryern Arcade and Safeway. A new 'mall' of shops has also been built at Fryern Hill during the last decade, leading to the new library, which celebrated its tenth anniversary in 1993.

In 1960, a new Anglican church, St Martin's in the Wood, was built to accommodate the people of the Hiltingbury area, and the church of St Francis now serves the new Valley Park development. St Martin's has recently been modernised and extended, as has St Boniface,

St Edward's, and the United Reformed church (previously Congregational). The Methodist congregation moved into new all-purpose premises on Winchester Road in 1957, and this was followed by the building of a new church in 1969. In 1993, this complex of buildings was refurbished, modernised and extended.

What, then, has become of that stretch of countryside described at the beginning of this introduction? Much of it has disappeared under the constant building programme, but Eastleigh Borough Council, Hampshire Wildlife Trust and the Woodland Trust are responsible for the conservation and management of several acres of remaining woodland and wet meadow.

These areas continue to provide not only a valuable habitat for the many species of wildlife for which they are a home, but also a constant source of challenge, interest and relaxation for the human inhabitants of Chandler's Ford, both newcomer and native.

From Countryside to Suburbia

1. Hocombe Road is the northern boundary of Chandler's Ford. This photograph was taken in 1899.

2. Taken in 1899, this photograph shows the junction of Lakewood Road and Hocombe Road, looking westwards.

3. The view, looking eastwards along Hocombe Road, in 1899.

4. Bisecting the wooded area between Hiltingbury Road and Hocombe Road was open land, known as Hocombe Meadows.

5. This photograph, taken in 1924, shows the two tracks, which have become the junction of Oakwood Road and Hiltingbury Road, for many hundreds of years an area of heathland and woodland. Here, Bronze Age men buried their dead, and Second World War troops camped prior to D-Day.

6. Pine woods were a feature of the Chandler's Ford landscape, frequently mentioned in documents and advertisements of Victorian and Edwardian times.

7. This is the area of land at Hiltingbury on which Ashdown Road, the shops and the *Tabby Cat* public house now stand. This Hiltingbury heathland was formerly home to nightjars, stonechats and other heathland species.

8. These gravel pits, of which there were a number in the Chandler's Ford area, were on the present site of Hiltingbury recreation ground.

9. Many woodland tracks have now become residential roads. This is Lakewood Road in 1899.

10. Lakewood Road, looking north from its junction with Hiltingbury Road.

11. Lakewood Road was one of the first 'woodland' roads in which one or two substantial houses began to appear in the first part of the 20th century.

12. This was the scene in 1899, looking northwards along Hursley Road, from its junction with Hiltingbury Road.

13. Hiltingbury Cottage stood on the corner of Hiltingbury Road and Hursley Road. One of the advertised attractions when it was for sale in 1899 was the singing of nightingales in the nearby woodland.

14. In 1928, the land surrounding the big house, Merdon, situated in what is now Merdon Avenue, was sold, and Kingsway was developed with housing. Kingsway post office, on the corner of Kingsway and Hiltingbury Road, was opened in 1930, and run by Miss Matilda Carter.

15. This photograph shows the point at which Queens Road joins Lakewood Road. It was taken in 1899.

16. Mrs. Goater moved into a new house in Hiltingbury Road in the early 1930s. This photograph, taken in 1935, shows her two sons with their grandmother, on the track through the woods which is now Queens Road.

17. Fryern Hill, 1903. The shop on the corner of what is now Oakmount Road was a baker's shop which also served teas. The *Halfway Inn* was built in 1870.

18. A view of Fryern Hill in 1908.

19. Taken just before the First World War, this shows a group of children on The Green at Fryern Hill, now the site of Safeways. The Green was an open space, with trees and scrub, and a small pond.

20. The bay windows were added to the *Halfway Inn* in 1912, and when this photograph was taken in 1914, the house on the corner of Brownhill Road, now Brownhill surgery, had been built.

21. By the 1920s, some motor cars and lorries had begun to use the main Winchester-Southampton road, passing through Fryern Hill.

22. The Wide-Awake Café can just be seen on this 1940s photograph.

23. This photograph of Fryern Hill was taken about 1950, and shows the shops on the right which were built in the 1930s.

24. Houses were built in Valley Road, seen here from its junction with Park Road, during the late 19th and early 20th centuries.

25. Crescent Road, now Merdon Avenue, was a long, winding, tree-lined road, with just one or two substantial houses built at the turn of the century.

26. These bungalows and houses, opposite the present entrance to Merdon Junior school, were built just before Crescent Road changed its name to Merdon Avenue in 1932, when Chandler's Ford became part of the borough of Eastleigh. This was done to avoid confusion with The Crescent in Eastleigh itself.

27. The shops on the left, known as the Parade, in Bournemouth Road, were built in the 1930s, and consisted of a butcher, baker, radio and electrical service, National Provincial Bank, grocer, ladies' hairdresser, wines and spirits shop, ladies' outfitter, and a fishmonger.

28. Shaftesbury Avenue was one of the roads developed off Bournemouth Road in the 1930s, after the sale of the land of Hut Farm.

29. Chalvington Road was developed during the 1930s. This photograph was taken at its junction with Leigh Road. The garage was built between the two world wars.

30. This aerial view was taken in 1950, just before the concentrated development following the Second World War had begun.

The Fords of Chandler's Ford

31. Until the 1920s the ford in Leigh Road had only a footbridge. All vehicles still had to go through the ford. It is a mile or so from the 'centre' of Chandler's Ford, and is, therefore, not considered to be the ford from which the village was named.

32. The ford at the junction of Park Road and Hursley Road had a bridge before the beginning of the century. However, it was a common occurrence during wet winters for the brook to flood at this point. The photograph, taken in 1960, shows the last time that this happened, much work having now been done on the banks of the brook to prevent any further flooding.

33. The car in this 1920s photograph has just crossed the bridge which marks the site of the ford on the main Winchester-Southampton road, a point just to the north of the present Central Shopping Precinct.

Interesting Buildings and Their People

34. Hiltonbury Farm, although built at the end of the 16th century, has had many additions and extensions. In the 1930s, a room was found, the existence of which had not been suspected for it had been locked up for many years. The last farmer at Hiltonbury, Mr. John Vining, was a descendant of the Beattie family who had farmed there for more than eighty years.

35. Mr. John Vining and his family. Mr. Vining's grandfather, Mr. Simon Beattie, had the named changed to Hiltonbury rather than Hiltingbury, in order to change postal districts from Winchester to Bishopstoke so that his mail would be delivered, rather than having to be collected from Hursley.

36. This early 17th-century cottage was situated at the top of Ramalley Lane, where the Headquarters of the 2nd Chandler's Ford Scout Group now stands. This is where, for 200 years, the annual 'merrie feasts' were held.

37. Originally two of the Ramalley cottages, made into one house after the Second World War, called Willow Thatch. It was demolished about ten years ago. In 1740, the families rented these cottages for five shillings per annum.

38. This is the only remaining thatched cottage within the Chandler's Ford boundary. It is situated in Cuckoo Bushes Lane.

39. Ford Farm, in Hursley Road, has now become part of a small modern development called Fortune Court, which is named after the Fortune family who were the last farmers at Ford Farm.

40. King's Court, now the Masonic headquarters, was built in 1894 by Mr. and Mrs. Wallis. This view looks across the lawns towards the terrace.

41. The driveway and the main entrance to King's Court. Behind King's Court was King's Lane, part of the legendary route by which the body of William Rufus was taken to Winchester for burial by Purkess, a charcoal burner. It was the subject of a right of way dispute in the 1890s between Mr. Wallis and another Mr. Purkess, who won the case.

42. The entrance hall, staircase and stained-glass window which still greets visitors to King's Court.

43. The lodge stood at the gateway into King's Court. The gateposts can still be seen, and the lodge has been extended to form the King's Court Restaurant, known in the 1930s as the King's Court Roadhouse.

44. The staff at King's Court, just before the First World War.

45. Merdon was another big house built in the early years of this century and situated at the end of what is now Merdon Close. After the sale of much of its land between the wars, Merdon became St Faith's Nursing Home, until it was demolished after the Second World War.

46. The original St Faith's Nursing Home was situated on Bournemouth Road, opposite Selwood's.

47. Merrieleas survives and has been converted into flats. Merrieleas Drive and Merrieleas Close have been built on what were the grounds of the house.

48. These farmworkers' cottages at Fryern Hill stood on the present site of the library. They were demolished in the 1950s.

49. This house stood where cars now enter Fryern Arcade. Between the wars, it was altered and extended to form the Wide-Awake Café. The family in the photograph is the Savory family, the last people to live in the house.

50. Fern Hill Cottages, built in 1882.

51. Eva Harris, aged eight in this photograph, was born at Fern Hill cottages in 1915. When she was 11, she became the first pupil to pass the scholarship examination from the Chandler's Ford Senior School, which enabled her to continue her education at Barton Peveril Grammar School.

52. This house stood on the present site of the National Westminster Bank. Built in 1909, it was bought by Mr. and Mrs. H. G. Hillier, who called it 'Henley' after a small hamlet in the area of Dorset, from which the family had come. Mr. and Mrs. Hillier were founder members of the Primitive Methodist chapel in Chandler's Ford.

53. Lou Meadon moved into Chandler's Ford's first council houses built at Fryern Hill in the 1920s. She was a well-known figure in the village, whose home reflected her 'unmodernised' lifestyle, including a kitchen range, in use until the day she finally moved to an old people's home in the early 1980s.

54. Chandler's Ford's first post office was at the end of a terrace in Bournemouth Road, opposite the *Hut Hotel*.

55. The terrace in which the post office was situated was built in the 19th century to house the brickworkers. This photograph, taken between the wars, shows Mrs. Biddlecombe and her son. The family still live in the same house.

56. The *Hut Hotel* was built in the 1890s on Bournemouth Road.

57. This wedding group of 1908 is taken outside the couple's new home on the Bournemouth Road, the houses having been built a few years before. The couple were married at Ampfield church by the Rev. Vere Awdry, father of the creator of Thomas the Tank Engine. St Boniface church was not licensed for marriages until 1910.

58. This house, called 'Baywood', on Bournemouth Road was the home of Mr. A. T. Higgins, Superintendent for Roads and Bridges for Hampshire County Council in the 1930s. The boy in the photograph is his son.

59. When it was first built on the corner of Hursley Road in 1900, this was Chandler's Ford's post office. It later became the offices of the Gas Company, and then belonged to R. and K. Martin (electricians) until it was demolished in 1984, for road widening. The girl in the immediate foreground is now Mrs. Gregory (aged 86) who still lives in Chandler's Ford.

60. The Ritchie Hall was opened in April 1914, having been built as a memorial to Dr. Ritchie, a local physician for 15 years. It became the focal point for many social events in the village, and the present Community Association rooms have been built next to it, forming one complex.

61. The Central Club and Institute was built in the 1920s and served as a recreational club for the working men of the village.

62. This photograph taken in 1910, looking northwards along Hursley Road, shows the *Railway Hotel*, and a small building on the extreme right, which was the reading room.

63. Built in 1900, as the Hursley Union Workhouse, this building became a sanatorium for tuberculosis patients in 1921, and is now Leigh House, a psychiatric unit.

Transport, Trade and Industry

64. Chandler's Ford railway station was opened in 1847, and in its early days was used mainly by the family from Hursley Park House. In February 1848, Lady Selina Heathcote wrote in her diary, 'Sir William went up to Town from Chandler's Ford Station, now recently opened'.

65. This view, taken from the station in 1905, and looking towards the entrance, shows the *Railway Hotel*, now the *Monk's Brook*, which was built in 1898.

66. Brick-making was an important industry in Chandler's Ford from the 1870s until the First World War. This group of men worked in the largest brickyard, which stretched from the railway, along Bournemouth Road, almost to Castle Lane.

67. This view of the station, taken early this century, shows the single-track railway which ran through the brickyard, for easy transportation of the bricks.

68. Mr. Ames was the stationmaster at Chandler's Ford in the 1930s.

69. The Snowball Laundry was opened in 1898. It was situated in Park Road, and this photograph shows one of the laundry vans in the 1920s. The gentleman is Mr. John Dowell, who designed the picture on the side of the van.

70. The laundry vans in the 1930s and '40s advertised the laundry as 'the Laundry in the Country'. Destroyed by fire in 1958, the laundry was rebuilt and continued as the Chantex Laundry, then Initial Services, and has only recently been demolished for the building of a small housing development.

71. The staff at the laundry, enjoying a lunchtime game of cricket.

72. Mr. A. H. Wadden was District Superintendent of the London and South Western Railway. He lived at Preston Pans Villa in Bournemouth Road, which is now the offices for Reynolds Parkhurst. The photograph was taken to celebrate the acquisition of his new pony and trap.

73. Interest in motoring grew in the 1920s and '30s. Mr. Wadden is seated in the rear of the car, his niece, Miss Florence Wadden, being in the driving seat.

74. In the 1920s, one of Chandler's Ford's first garages was built at Fryern Hill, where Safeways is now situated. It was known as the South Hants Motor Engineering Works, and Mr. J. F. Gorst was the proprietor.

75. In 1928, in the interests of road safety, the Parish Council suggested a 10 m.p.h. speed limit through the village. Mr. M. Horn, an early motorist, would have had to adhere to this.

76. The original shop from which this building developed, was recorded in the 1841 census and was the earliest shop in Chandler's Ford. Originally kept as a general shop by Mr. Ham Rodaway, the building was developed and extended into two shops, and ended its life as an off-licence called The Cottage. The Circle K shop in Oakmount Road now occupies this site.

77. This early 20th-century photograph of Hursley Road shows the general 'corner shop' on the corner of Common Road. The houses on the left were built in 1898, but the shop was there before that date and has remained to the present day.

78. Mr. Albert Dean began his coal, corn and seed merchant's business in 1906 in this shop in Hursley Road, one of a pair on the corner of Ramalley Lane. It is now the offices of Laishley's, the builders.

79. Mr. Albert Dean, his wife, family and horse, Prince, which was kept in a field just off Hursley Road.

80. Mr. Dean's son, Mr. F. H. Dean, continued the business as has his son, Mr. Roger Dean. In the 1930s, they moved to the present premises in Hursley Road, this photograph showing the original building, before post-war extensions and additions.

81. This was the first lorry used by Mr. F. H. Dean. Deliveries in the early days were made by horse and cart.

82. This photograph shows the rear of Mr. F. H. Dean's premises, with the early delivery lorries. Both photographs date from the 1930s.

83. The first newsagent's shop in the village was the building on the right of this photograph, on the corner of Park Road and Hursley Road. It was run by Mr. Pook.

84. This row of shops at the end of Hursley Road contained a Co-op and the first bank in the village (Lloyds). The shops were never properly completed due to the outbreak of the First World War.

85. Familiar to all those who lived at Fryern Hill, prior to and following the Second World War, was Munckton's grocery shop, on the corner of Oakmount Road. This photograph was taken at Christmas 1934, and shows Mr. Munckton in his shop.

86. This photograph shows the exterior of Mr. Munckton's shop.

87. Just after the Second World War, Mr. William Selwood began his Plant Hire and Engineering business in the building which had been the Senior School. New premises were gradually developed and the school building was demolished in 1984.

88. The firm of Selwood, demonstrating to Mr. F. H. Dean the latest machinery to facilitate the unloading of coal from the railway trucks.

Churches

89. St Boniface church, as it looked when it was first opened in 1904.

90. St Boniface church, 1930. The addition of the chancel and the installation of the organ were dedicated on 15 December 1929.

91. A group in costume for a church festival held at St Boniface in 1912.

92. The interior of St Boniface church in 1930.

93. Miss Eva and Miss Edith Harris show the bridesmaids' fashion of the day at their sister, Mabel Elizabeth's, wedding, held at St Boniface church in August 1933.

94. The Primitive Methodist chapel, on the right of this photograph, was opened in November 1900, in Brownhill Road. It is now the Age Concern Hall, ceasing to be the chapel, when new premises were built on Winchester Road, in 1957.

95. *(Top left)* Methodist Harvest Festival in 1912. At the front are two of the founder members: Mr. H. G. Hillier on the right, and his eldest son, Mr. F. W. Hillier, on the left.

96. *(Left)* A group at the Methodist chapel in 1916, showing some of the adult members and children of the Sunday School. Mr. W. H. Hillier, the soldier on the left, was killed in action in France, shortly after this photograph was taken.

97. *(Top right)* The Methodist chapel, decorated for Harvest Festival in the 1930s by Mr. F. R. Castle, who owned the Fryern Hill Nurseries. He was the father of the late Lord Castle, and the father-in-law of Lady Barbara Castle.

98. The Methodist worshippers celebrating the stone-laying of the new extension to their chapel in 1936.

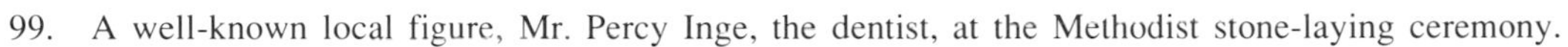

99. A well-known local figure, Mr. Percy Inge, the dentist, at the Methodist stone-laying ceremony.

100. The extension of the Methodist chapel was of great benefit to the Sunday School. This photograph was taken in 1937, on the first Sunday that the new room was used. At the back is Mr. H. M. Hillier, who had just succeeded his father as Sunday School Superintendent.

101. The 4th Chandler's Ford Guide Company, based at the Methodist church and founded in 1938 by Mrs. R. F. Dore, who can be seen on the left of the photograph.

102. The Congregational church, in King's Road, was built under the leadership of the Rev. Lloyd Jones, a retired minister, who began by holding services in his house. The church was opened on 17 October 1929.

103. Taken shortly before the official opening, this photograph shows the Congregational church with its founder, the Rev. Lloyd Jones, and its first minister, the Rev. Dennis Cooper.

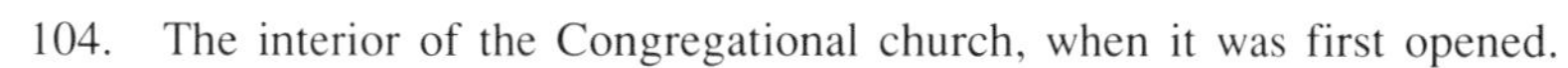

104. The interior of the Congregational church, when it was first opened.

105. Harvest Supper in the new hall of the Congregational church, 1934.

106. A young people's outing from the Congregational church in the 1930s, with the Rev. Parnaby, the minister.

Schools

107. This school was built in 1893 on Bournemouth Road. After the Infant School was built in King's Road in 1908, it became the 'Senior School' for pupils aged nine to fourteen.

108. A school group of the 1890s, with Mrs. Cleall, the headteacher, in the centre.

109. The new Infant School in King's Road was opened in 1908. Miss Bennett was the first headteacher, but she was soon succeeded by Miss Goulding, who remained in her post until after the Second World War.

110. A group of pupils at the Infant School in King's Road in 1916.

111. One of the Infant School classrooms in 1916, with Miss Goulding, the headteacher, sitting at the desk.

112. Pupils at the Infant School in the 1920s, clearly showing the classroom furniture of the day.

113. This photograph was taken at the Infant School, at the time of the First World War.

114. Empire Day, 1910. The Senior School used its new flag for the first time.

115. A group of pupils at the Senior School in 1916.

116. A Senior School group in 1921, with Mr. Howse, the headteacher, on the left of the photograph.

School
1922-3

117. *(Top left)* The Senior School football team of 1922-23. The teacher in charge is Mr. Lush.

118. *(Left)* A photograph of Miss Andrews' class of 1926-27.

119. *(Top right)* The school choir of the Chandler's Ford Senior School in 1931, after winning the shield for being one of the best school choirs in Hampshire. The choirmaster, Mr. Lush, can be seen at the back, on the right of the photograph.

120. Mrs. Wise founded Sherborne House School in 1932, and the original building was in Park Road. The school moved to its current premises in Lakewood Road in 1935, when this photograph was taken.

121. This photograph dating from 1934 shows a group of the first pupils to attend Sherborne House School.

122. Sherborne House School's Guides and Brownies, taken in 1946.

Sport and Recreation

123. One of the earliest photographs of Chandler's Ford Football Club. This was the team of 1895-96. *Back row*: W. Calen, S. Mitchener, J. Whitter, G. Draper, H. Mead and A. B. Roker. *Middle row*: A. Witts, F. K. Holme, S. White, W. Purkess and H. Draper. *Front row*: J. Chappell and D. Smith.

124. Chandler's Ford United Football Club, 1907-8. During this season they were winners of the Winchester and District League and the Andover Village Tournament. They were also runners-up in the Salisbury Junior Tournament, and winners and runners-up in the Eastleigh League Junior Tournament. This photograph is of particular interest as it incudes Dr. Ritchie who was the Honorary Treasurer.

125. Chandler's Ford Football Club 1910-11. In this season, they were the winners of the London and South Western Railway Orphanage Cup and the Andover Village Tournament.

126. Chandler's Ford Football Club in the 1921-22 season.

127. The football team which represented Chandler's Ford at the beginning of the Second World War.

128. Chandler's Ford Rifle Club 1911-12. They were winners of the 2nd Division of the Southampton and District League. *Back row*: W. H. Carpenter, A. Musselwhite, R. Betteridge, F. Ford, W. S. Naylor and G. A. Beattie. *Middle row*: F. Curtis, H. Bailey, H. Bray (Capt.), F. Legg and A. Smith. *Front row*: C. Hooper and W. Legg.

129. Fryern Hill Cricket Club 1911, one of Chandler's Ford's earliest cricket teams.

130. Chandler's Ford Cricket Club played for many years on a ground on the corner of Hursley Road and Baddesley Road. Part of the North Miller's Dale housing estate has now been built upon it. This photograph shows the 1922 team who played on that ground.

131. The Chandler's Ford Brass and Reed Band was formed before the First World War, and it performed at various village fairs and functions.

132. Schoolgirls dancing at a village fête in 1914.

133. A meeting of the Hursley Hunt was of great interest to the villagers. The meet sometimes took place at the *Hut Hotel*, but this photograph, taken in 1907, is outside the *Halfway Inn* at Fryern Hill.

134. The villagers of Chandler's Ford would have travelled a little further afield to attend the Hursley point-to-point races in 1913.

135. At Chandler's Ford's first carnival, held in 1919, this entry was billed as the 'Darkie Wedding', 'blacking up' being an acceptable and popular form of entertainment at that time.

136. At the carnival judging, the 'Darkie Wedding' won first prize.

137. A part of the first carnival procession as it passed through Fryern Hill.

138. Mr. Bunce's lorry was used for delivering coal, as a float in carnival processions, and, with the addition of seats on the back, as an early 'bus' to Eastleigh, before the Hants and Dorset Bus Company began their regular service in 1920.

139. In 1921, this was the carnival entry of the Chandler's Ford Women's Institute, which had been started by Miss Kennedy, who can be seen on the right of the photograph. The entry was entitled 'For home and industry', and showed the various articles which the Institute taught its members to make.

140. The annual carnival finished with a fair which was held in a field at Hut Farm. This photograph was taken in 1924.

141. The lake at Chandler's Ford, which may have originated as ancient fish ponds, has continued to be a site of relaxation for the villagers.

142. This skating party of 1912 took advantage of the lake being frozen over.

143. *(Top left)* Skating again took place on the lake in the 1930s.

144. *(Left)* Mrs. Hignett started the first Brownies and Girl Guides in Chandler's Ford in 1920. She had a hut built in the garden of her house, 'Garth', in Lakewood Road, in which the meetings were held.

145. *(Top right)* May time in the 1920s. A group of children at the Senior School ready to perform the popular Maypole Dance.

146. Proud mothers with their babies at a baby show held in 1921.

147. A group of members of the Chandler's Ford and Eastleigh Cycling Club, 1943-44.

Wartime Memories

148. The celebratory procession held in 1919, to mark the end of the First World War. The procession has come from the Ritchie Hall, is passing the *Railway Hotel*, and is about to proceed to a field at Hut Farm for further celebrations. The event was spread over two occasions, as torrential rain brought the first to an untimely conclusion.

149. The children of the village dressed in costumes of different countries to celebrate the end of the First World War.

150. The War Memorial was erected in March 1920.

151. At first the War Memorial stood at the end of Hursley Road, but has now been moved to a site outside St Boniface church.

152. A parade of naval cadets, about to enter Bournemouth Road from Leigh Road. The parade took place in 1935.

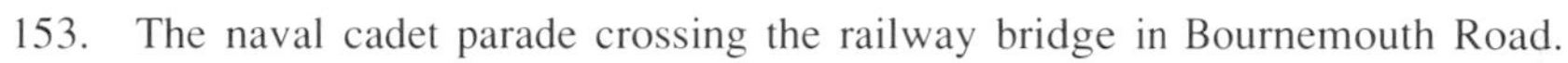

153. The naval cadet parade crossing the railway bridge in Bournemouth Road.

154. This gallant band of men formed Chandler's Ford's Home Guard in 1940.

155. The Home Guard preparing for action.

156. Shooting practice for members of the Home Guard on what is now the Flexford Nature Reserve.

157. The local Civil Defence Group in the Second World War.

158. The residents of Fryern Hill celebrated the end of the Second World War at the Methodist chapel.

159. A street party held by the residents of Bournemouth Road to celebrate the end of the war.

Finally

160. To mark the beginning of a new era in the life of the country and the development of Chandler's Ford, residents of Fryern Hill celebrate the coronation of H.M. Queen Elizabeth II, at the *Halfway Inn*.